I Know How to Lose Weight, So Why Haven't I

Lisa M Evans, MA, CDP

Marquise Publishing · Cleveland, Ohio

I Know How to Lose Weight, So Why Haven't I
By Lisa M Evans, MA, CDP
Published by:
Marquise Publishing
11459 Mayfield Rd., Suite 338
Cleveland, Ohio 44106 U.S.A.

lisamevansceo@gmail.com

http://lmeceo.com

All rights reserved. No part of this book may be reproduced or transmitted in any form or by any means, electronic or mechanical, including photocopying, recording or by any information storage and retrieval system, without written permission from the author, except for the inclusion of brief quotations in a review.

Unattributed quotations are by Lisa M Evans

Copyright 2016; 2021

ISBN 978-0-9745264-6-1

Printed in the United States of America

Contents

About the Author
Preface-Note to Reader
Acknowledgements
Warning- Disclaimer
Introduction

I Know *How* to Lose Weight

1 Pep talk	15
2 Tell me something I don't know	19
3 Bad habits	23
4 Prioritize/Planning	31
5 Getting back to basics	39
6 Get moving	59
7 Love ourselves now	71

So *Why* Haven't I?

8 What's really going on	79
9 Mind games	95
10 The quick fix	101
11 Looking good=feeling good	107
12 Maintenance	111
Afterword	115
Glossary	119
Index	123
Colophon	125

About the Author

Lisa M Evans, MA, CDP is a mother of two lovely daughters. A fan of classic Hip Hop she writes poems to satisfy her inner MC. She wrote her first book about a lonely hat at the age of six. Lisa is an alumnus of Cleveland State University where she earned her Master's degree in psychology and certification in Diversity Management.

Lisa has recognized that most people know how to lose weight, but still find themselves struggling to achieve a healthy lifestyle. Unhealthy body image and mental mind games can contribute to one developing bad habits that undermine lifestyle changes. Her own personal experiences with these issues prompted her to write this book.

To keep up with Lisa's journey and get further information on adopting a healthy lifestyle follow her blog www.lmeceo.com.

It is the goal of Lisa Evans and Marquise Publishing to provide quality reading material for informational and entertainment purposes.

Note to the Reader

The diet and weight loss industry is a billion dollar business. Every pill, powder, and gizmo on the market has consumers looking for a magic solution to weight loss. The truth is most of us **know** how to lose weight, but struggle to do so. Maintaining a healthy lifestyle is more than physical. Mental, emotional and, even spiritual factors play a major influence.

There is not enough room to include everything you should know about nutrition and weight loss. It is best practice to consult a professional and do your own research for information outside of the information provided in this book.

Lisa M Evans, Cleveland, OH

Acknowledgments

I would like to thank God for his many blessings.
I dedicate this book to my daughters, Alexis and Alonna, the loves of my life. To Alissa and La Toya, I am truly blessed to have you in my life, thank you for believing in me; and to my sister, Teresa, for being there for me in my time of need.

I sincerely thank all of the fine people that have contributed to this book. I know they are as proud as I am of the work they helped to create.

Warning-Disclaimer

This book is designed to provide information on exercise, basic nutrition, emotional and mental issues. It is sold with the understanding that the publisher and author are not engaged in rendering medical, dietetic, psychiatric, or other professional services. If medical, mental, or other expert assistance is required, the services of a competent professional should be sought. As with anything dealing with lifestyle changes, please consult your physician before implementing any of the suggestions in this book.

It is not the purpose of this book to reprint all the information that is otherwise available to those seeking knowledge on better nutrition, weight loss, and mental health, but to complement, and supplement other texts. You are urged to read all the available material, learn as much as possible about nutrition, weight loss, and wellness.

Every effort has been made to make this book as complete and as accurate as possible. However, there may be mistakes, both typographical and in content. Therefore this text should be used only as a general guide and not as the ultimate source of lifestyle change and wellness information. Furthermore, this book contains information that is current only up to the printing date.

The purpose of this book is to educate and entertain. The author and Marquise Publishing shall have neither liability nor responsibility to any person or entity with respect to any loss or damage caused, or alleged to have been caused, directly or indirectly, by the information contained in this book.

If you do not wish to be bound by the above, you may return this book to the publisher for a full refund.

Introduction

Was there ever a time in your life you were physically active on a consistent basis, ate a well balanced clean diet, felt an overall sense of well being?

At one point in my life that was me. I injured my ankle and it prevented me from working out. I went into a deep depression and started on a 7 month junk food binge. After gaining a lot of weight I tried to get back to where I was before I hurt my ankle.

I put myself under a lot of pressure to return to my previous weight, so I was working out harder than I did before. I became frustrated with the fact that I was working out so diligently and so hard, but could not get back to my previous weight. I eventually gave up and gave into bad habits.

I realize that I am only focusing on one element of leading a healthy lifestyle. Although I had exercised regularly, I didn't eat properly or drink enough water to sustain my physical activity. I kept late hours and I had gotten into the bad habit of functioning on very little sleep

After being inactive for months, the thought of starting over and getting back to working out on a regular basis has me hesitant to get started. Honestly, I don't want to have to work that hard.

Along with my hesitation to exercise, there is another set of factors I have to deal with. Emotionally, I have been struggling with bouts of insecurity and doubts about whether I could get motivated to make changes in my health as well as in my life.

Mentally, I have all these responsibilities and worries that are taking space in my brain. This, in turn, causes me to scrap the whole idea of trying to get fit and wait for a better time to get started on me.

This is the point where I looked at myself in a full length mirror and changed my entire disposition.
Procrastination is no longer an option. I have to start now, and I have to do something to improve the way I feel both mentally and physically.

I am no different than anyone else. I want maximum results with minimum effort. I am also realistic and accept that there has to be some earnest investment on my part if I want to be healthy.

So this time around I looked at some of the mistakes I made in the past when I was working toward my fitness goals, and examined all the elements needed to get results and maintain results without killing myself in the process.

To achieve this goal, I have created a strategy that involves all the important components for overall health and well-being.

I examined basic components to weight loss that have stood the test of time, and learned that change is not going to happen overnight.

I looked at:

- How to incorporate more physical activities in my daily routine, and eventually work my way to a full-blown exercise schedule.

- Bad habits that are known to ruin anyone's figure, and ways to incorporate good habits that will become routine.

- Emotional factors such as: stress, procrastination, and depression. These emotions, if allowed to get out of hand can wreak havoc in our lives as well as our bodies.

I feel this approach is the best way to achieve overall well-being that will not only change my body, but my mind and spirit as well.

I decided to write this book as I may be able to help someone else that is having a similar struggle.

I want you, the reader, to love yourself and really address whether you need to or want to lose weight and for what reasons. If you want to be your best self, it doesn't take killing yourself to do it.

I Know **How** to Lose Weight

14 I Know How to Lose Weight, So Why Haven't I?

1

Pep talk

Maybe this is the umpteenth New Year's resolution we have made, or we ran into an old friend who looks great and has politely brought to our attention that we have gained a few pounds (as if we did not notice), or we are at the point where we are just tired of being tired and are ready to make a change. Whatever the reason, we have decided this time to do something about our weight.

Right now we are feeling empowered, motivated, and ready to tackle the problem head on. One glance in the mirror and the empowerment turns to helplessness. The motivation becomes doubt. The will to tackle the problem becomes fear of failure. So we give in to that negative voice in our head and convince ourselves we are doomed to be unhealthy forever.

We have all been there. This is the hardest place to be emotionally and physically. This is the crossroad where we either take action or continue down our current path. If we choose to take action, take a deep breath, look in the mirror, and make a pact to start working toward improving our health. Remember it took time to get where we are and it will take time to get where we want to be.

Weight loss is as much of an emotional process as a physical one. Changes in our mood and overall feeling of well-being can affect our attitude toward ourselves and affect our weight loss efforts.

We must start by being honest with ourselves and trust our own abilities to create an environment for change. Weight loss requires a change in lifestyle. This change should be as routine as brushing our teeth. Anything that is approached under stress, anxiety, or with unrealistic expectations will be impossible to maintain.

The key is to approach lifestyle change armed with a strategic well thought-out plan of action. What are our goals? How will we work toward them? Take a look at our lives as a whole. Is our current weight a result of a tragedy or setback in our career, relationship, or have we made ourselves into a physical shield against pain or discomfort we may be dealing with. The way we treat or mistreat our bodies is usually a manifestation of how well we are coping with our emotions and our environment.

The process is going to take time, commitment and consistency. We will take a holistic approach to developing our strategy and pinpoint those areas that need improvement or are roadblocks to our success. We will review our thought processes and unlearn the quick-fix and go for the slow and steady route to lifestyle change.

We will learn to trust ourselves and get back in touch with our bodies. We will learn how to incorporate common sense in our decisions about food and exercise to avoid setting ourselves up for failure. We will learn to enjoy life in our own bodies on our own terms.

There will never be a perfect time for change. We can come up with millions of excuses why we should put ourselves on hold and wait for a better time to start.

Pep talk

The planets will not come into alignment. The sky will not open and cast a beam of light engulfing us to let us know the time is right. Time will pass whether we change or not. If we want to change - the time is now.

18   I Know How to Lose Weight, So Why Haven't I?

2

Tell me something I don't know

Ok let's be real here. Losing weight is not some mysterious event that only occurs when we wish on a falling star and click our heels together three times, there's no place like size 0. Most of us know our bodies and know what we have to do in order to lose weight. It's the challenges and roadblocks some of us encounter on the road to a healthier lifestyle that lead us to question our methods and seek help from other sources (reliable and unreliable).

The challenges to adopting a healthier lifestyle for some of us seem to be:

- Getting started
- Being consistent
- Maintenance

Some of these challenges have nothing to do with diet and exercise, but with our thoughts and feelings toward weight loss and body image that are influenced by how we perceive ourselves, and how we handle our environment.

So unlike other books that deal with the subject of lifestyle change, this book is:

- For the procrastinator
- For the person who resolves to lose weight every New Year, does well for two months, then falls off the wagon and gains it all back plus some
- For the person who spends hundreds of dollars on a weight loss boot camp that has no maintenance plan other than to sign up for more boot camps
- For the person who dreads the thought of going to the gym
- For the person who wants to lose weight and lead a healthier lifestyle, but has anxiety on how to start
- For the person who passes on going out with friends because they don't like the way they look in their clothes
- For the person who doesn't want to starve themselves to lose weight
- For the person who believes losing weight is going to magically change their life
- For the person who wants to make a lifestyle change
- For you

This book addresses more than just diet and exercise; it suggests other wellness factors to consider when developing a plan for success.

It takes a holistic approach to lifestyle change. The beginning goes over the basics that we all know need to be implemented in any successful plan, the latter part of the book dives a little deeper and addresses issues that are not always considered.

This book doesn't promote:

- Get slim quick techniques
- Fad diet plans
- A one-size-fits-all-approach
- A way around proper nutrition and exercise
- A diet pill or weight loss shake

So if you are at a point in your life where making excuses no longer works for you...

then now is the time to do something different, and this is the book to help you do it.

Now you have a choice to make. Continue to do what you've been doing, or make reasonable changes and focus on undoing some of your bad habits and start down the road of change.

Choose the latter.

22 I Know How to Lose Weight, So Why Haven't I?

3

Bad habits

Positive changes take more conscious effort than negative ones, but negative ones have greater consequences.

A habit is defined as a recurrent, often unconscious pattern of behavior that is acquired through frequent repetition.

Many habits that we have developed like brushing our teeth, paying bills on time, getting to appointments on time are considered to be good and help contribute to the ease and efficiency of living.

What bad habits have we developed over time that has contributed to our current weight? Do we eat only one meal a day or eat a large meal before bed? Do we skip breakfast? Drink too much caffeine, alcohol or consume a lot of liquid calories? All of these bad habits, singly or in any combination, can contribute to weight gain.

Late Night Eating
Eating large meals right before bed is probably one of the easiest ways to pack on the pounds. Eating late at night interferes with our sleep (i.e. gas, nightmares, discomfort) and adds extra calories that our bodies do not process efficiently end up and storing them instead. Our last meal of the day should be at least 3 hours before bedtime.

Caffeine

Most people cannot start the day without a cup of Joe. It is something about the way freshly brewed coffee smells. Even in the summer heat, we see people with their iced coffees and lattes rushing to work.

There has been a lot said about caffeine both negative and positive. Caffeine is a mild stimulant. It is not addictive, but it can be habit forming. When people try to cut out caffeine cold turkey, they can experience headache, fatigue or drowsiness.

As with anything we put in our body, moderation is the key. A moderate intake of caffeine is 300 mg which equals about three 6oz cups of coffee.

A high consumption of caffeine can make us feel jittery and interfere with our sleeping patterns if consumed too close to bedtime. It is a mild diuretic and can aid in dehydration, especially in those who do not consume water on
a regular basis. Make sure to drink plenty of water when consuming caffeine.

Some people use caffeine to enhance energy levels. When trying to cut down or cut out caffeine from our diet try:
- Getting a good night's sleep
- Take a brisk walk
- Eat regular, healthy meals
- Do not eat large heavy meals - they tend to make us want to take a nap

The key to lowering or eliminating our caffeine intake is to gradually cut back. Try to reduce coffee or caffeinated beverages by a cup a day.

- Keep a log to see how much caffeine we consume (Include medications and supplements)
- Limit our intake to 200-300 mg of caffeine per day
- Try herbal tea or decaf coffee as substitutes
- Exercise and activity help increase energy levels naturally

- Stop smoking - caffeine and cigarettes often go together
- Replace coffee or caffeinated beverage with a glass of water
- Try a green smoothie or fruit smoothie in place of your morning cup of coffee

Liquid Calories
Liquid calories are easily overlooked when making healthy changes in our diet because they are not as obvious as food calories.
A 20oz bottle of cola is 100 calories per serving. There are 2.5 servings per bottle which equals 250 calories. Therefore when we want to cut unnecessary calories from our diet, liquid calories are the place to start.

Empty, high-calorie beverages are not filling, so adjustments are not often made when choosing to eat healthier. Some popular drinks are high in sugars that turn into fat that usually congregates around the midsection.

Specialty coffees like mocha fudge cappuccino can be 250-500 calories and contain up to 75grams of sugar per 20 oz serving.

Fruit drink mixes and concentrates are mostly water, flavoring, and sugar. Fruit drinks are not calorie dense, but have no nutritional value.

Sports drinks are good if we workout more than 90 minutes, especially in hot humid outdoor conditions because they contain electrolytes and carbohydrates. They also contain about 96 calories per 100ml.

Diet soft drinks contain zero calories because they use artificial sweeteners that may cause allergic reactions in some people.

Be aware that some diet soft drinks still contain caffeine, also we may tend to eat more because we feel like we are saving calories.

The acidity from the carbonation in most soft drinks is not good to consume in large quantities. It could cause bloating, acid reflux, and in some cases, can eat through the lining of our stomachs.

Alcohol consumption can sabotage any healthy eating plan. Hard liquors like gin, whisky brandy and vodka contain about 115 to 125 calories per shot. Mixed drinks can contain between 150 to 250 calories depending on the mixer used to make the drink. Wine has about 85 to 100 calories per 4oz glass and beer contains about 150 calories per 12oz bottle.
Alcohol lowers our inhibitions, stimulates appetite and contributes to weight gain in the abdomen. Limit alcohol consumption.

It is very important to take liquid calories and beverages with high sugar content into account when choosing to eat healthier.

Water is the best liquid to consume to quench our thirst.

Processed Foods
Processed foods are foods that have been altered from their natural state for convenience.
Processing methods include canning, freezing, refrigeration, and dehydration. Processed foods are made with trans fats, saturated fats, and large amounts of sodium and sugar. They're low in vitamins and minerals. Eating too much processed food is not healthy and contributes to weight gain. Some processed foods are made with chemicals in order to preserve their shelf life. When consumed in large quantities, these chemicals can have an adverse effect on our health beyond weight gain.

The following processed foods should be avoided:
- Canned foods with large amounts of sodium or fat

- Pasta meals made with refined white flour instead of whole grains
- Packaged high-calorie snack foods such as chips and candies
- Frozen dinners that are high in sodium
- Packaged cakes and cookies
- Boxed meal mixes that are high in fat and sodium
- Sugary breakfast cereals
- Processed meats
- Fast food

Avoid boxed, frozen, or shrink wrapped foods with ingredients that cannot be pronounced. Concentrate on whole, real, fresh foods.

Binging

We have all had those days when we get so busy that we go an entire day without eating, and we make up for the whole day in one meal. Or we are on a strict diet plan and as soon as we can go back to regular eating, we go on an eating spree.

Binging happens when we allow ourselves to go without eating for long periods of time or deprive ourselves of our favorite foods. Binging can also be a result of emotional eating or stress.

The act of stuffing in response to emotional or mental stress, this type of binging is merely a result of unresolved emotions that one is trying to satiate with food.

Binging is very detrimental to physical and mental well-being. Consuming a large amount of calories in one sitting is not good for digestion, and it messes up our metabolism. We can't make-up missed meals in one sitting.

If we are binging for emotional reasons, after the high from eating is gone, we are often left with feelings of shame and guilt; and the issue we are eating to ignore is still there.

To avoid binging:
- Try not to go more than 3 hours without eating
- Find healthy alternatives for our favorite foods to avoid total restriction of those foods.
- If we are experiencing emotional issues or stress, explore those feelings before reaching for food, seek professional help if necessary

S.W.B.
Snacking while bored. We have all done it - that phenomenon where our hands entertain our mouths with food in order to make time pass faster.

This is the time to take up a hobby like knitting or drawing. Consider that maybe we are really hungry and fix a healthy meal instead of going for an empty calorie snack. Maybe we are thirsty and should drink some water.

The next time we find ourselves mindlessly snacking stop, acknowledge that it is boredom and find a more productive way to occupy our time.

Public eating vs. private eating
We pack a light healthy lunch for work and order a salad or an entrée from the light section of the menu when out to dinner with friends, but when we are home alone, out come the chips and dip; and we order our favorite takeout from the restaurant we have on speed dial.

Does this sound familiar? It is easier to eat healthy and make better choices when we are around others that may hold us accountable for our food choices. However, if we find ourselves sabotaging those efforts with what we eat in private then there is no need to put up a healthy front.

It can be frustrating having co-workers and family members making comments about everything we put in our mouths, but it is better to eat what we want in public than to binge in private.

Bad habits

As the saying goes what's done in the dark will come to the light. What we eat in private will come to our hips, thighs, stomach, etc.

30   I Know How to Lose Weight, So Why Haven't I?

4

Prioritize/Planning

Make your journey easier by creating a roadmap to success.

Now it is time to develop a strategy that will incorporate healthy lifestyle changes.

Take the assessment on the next page.

Use this assessment to get a picture of where you are now and where you want to be.

Make a copy of the assessment and revisit it often to help you stay on track.

Answer the questions truthfully and really think about where you are.

Be realistic about goals and timeframes, you can always reassess.

Assessment

1. What is my current weight?
2. What is my goal weight?
3. How do I feel overall about starting a lifestyle change?
4. Am I ready to make a lifestyle change?
5. Emotional factors I'm dealing with.
6. Emotional factors I'm not dealing with.
7. Physical factors I'm dealing with.
8. Bad habits I feel are hindering my weight loss efforts.
9. Time of the day I have the most energy.
10. Number of days per week I have to devote to exercise
11. What does reaching my goal weight look and feel like?
12. Time frame I'm giving myself to reach my goal.
13. Is this timeframe realistic?
14. How motivated am I to reach this goal?

Visit a doctor and get a check-up to make sure there are no serious health problems. If there are, discuss specific and appropriate treatments, medications, and/or lifestyle changes we need to make.

Two weeks prior to beginning, any major changes to our routines, track our meals make a note of when we ate, what we ate, and why we ate. The amount of sleep we get each night, and the liquid calories we drink. Also, make note of the times of day in which we can increase our physical activity or get in a workout.

Set a primary goal and a date in the future to check our progress on the goal. There is really no end date to adopting a healthy lifestyle, so it is best to set check in dates to keep track of progress towards a goal. Be realistic about this check in date and allow enough time to develop the habit to achieve goal.

Remember, it took time to get where we are now, and it will take time to get where we want to be.

The goals that we set should contain all or some of the following components:

- Specific: Describe what we want to accomplish with as much detail as possible.

- Measurable: Describe our goal in terms that can clearly be evaluated.

- Challenging: Takes energy and discipline to accomplish.

- Realistic: A goal we know we are actually capable of obtaining.

- Stated Check in Date: Clearly specify completion dates for mini goals and your primary goal.

Once we have set our starting date, list the positive habits we want to develop and prioritize them in order of feasibility.

The objective is to plan a strategy for success and incorporate positive changes that will develop into good habits.

After the two weeks of tracking our meals, make a list of the foods we regularly eat. Include junk foods and high-calorie snacks. Make a note of how these foods are prepared and the time of day they are consumed.

The goal is to get an overall picture of the foods we consume during the day so we can see what areas need improvement and what foods need to be replaced with healthier ones.

How often should we eat?
The consensus is that we should eat every three to four hours. The core meals being breakfast, lunch and dinner with two or three snacks. This eating schedule keeps energy levels stabilized throughout the day and encourages proper metabolism of food. Try to plan meals and snacks for around the same time every day. By doing so, we will notice a significant change in our energy levels and mood; we will also see positive changes in our bodies.

Some say stick to three meals a day with no snacks in between. Do what feels best. The goal is to make sure we are eating clean, whole foods and are not mindlessly snacking or emotionally eating.

Take time to get our schedule to a point in which we are doing it without thinking about it.

Create a schedule and include the time we will wake up in the morning, the times of each meal and snack, the times for each activity or exercise, and the time we will go to bed. The goal is to create a basic guideline for our day; just remember to keep it realistic.

Keep a calendar
A calendar will not only give us a visual representation of our goals, but it will also help us track our progress and keep track of our milestones. Keep track of any appointments or commitments that may affect our schedule.

Don't plan more than two weeks in advance because:
- We don't want to overwhelm ourselves with a calendar full of workouts we may not be able to complete.

- We want to give ourselves room to make changes and adjustments to our routines.

Many of us lead very busy lives. When prioritizing our fitness goals, be aware that there may be days when things do not go according to schedule. Make the necessary adjustments and keep moving forward.

Planning meals
Meal planning helps to avoid binging and eating unhealthy foods. At the beginning of the week, plan, prepare and pack meals and snacks for the week. Invest in reusable containers, a water bottle, and a personal cooler.

Meal planning doesn't mean we can't eat out or grab lunch with co-workers. Plan for those meals too by looking at the menus of the restaurants online to see what healthy options they offer. Forego the appetizer or share it with the table. Drink water before your meal and only eat half of the portion you are served; box the other half for another meal.

Tracking your progress
The scale can't be trusted! The scale is not an accurate indicator of progress; don't be a slave to the scale. Instead, track progress through how we feel and how our clothes fit. Taking pictures as we go through our journey is a more accurate indication of progress than the scale is.

Bad days
There may be days when we have so much going on that there is no time to breathe. Those days are the ones we need to examine closely and figure out ways to lighten obligations.

Do not over schedule. If we have planned out our day, stick to the plan, and do not let feelings of guilt or false obligation persuade us take time away from our plan.

There are going to be times that we could care less about weight, exercising or anything else. In the past, days like this would have us running to the refrigerator or berating ourselves through negative self-talk or allowing ourselves to go into long periods of depression. Now we will take a different approach to these days.

- Acknowledge the emotion. Be upset, feel hurt, and cry if we want to.
- Write down our feelings. Writing them out will help release them and, in some cases, prevent us from lashing out at others.
- Put a time limit on negative emotions. Only allow a day or two (the more traumatic the event or situation, the more time we will allow) to feel negative emotions. Then, start the next day with a bright outlook and positive perspective on life in which we are refocused on reaching our goal.
- Once we have let go of the negativity, move on.

Seeking professional help
We all can use professional help, especially when it comes to making a lifestyle change. Don't be afraid to seek professional assistance in areas we know we struggle with. Make sure any professional we seek is certified and accredited.

- A psychologist can assist us in finding and uncovering the root causes of how we cope with stress and behaviors that may contribute to emotional eating.
- A nutritionist can assist us with making healthy food choices and put together meal plans to support our weight loss efforts.
- A personal trainer can provide motivation, some nutritional assistance and exercise routines to help us reach our wellness goals. The key to a good personal trainer is to find someone who listens and asks us about our current lifestyle and fitness goals. They should be someone who tailors a workout and nutrition plans to fit us and our goals.

As we get closer to our goal, less time will be spent actually thinking about the changes we are making. This is a good sign that we are forming good habits that are becoming more ingrained in our daily routine. As long as we are on track with our plan, the less work it takes to maintain.

Seven day challenges

To help us get started there will be seven day challenges included in the following chapters for some of the basic components of lifestyle change.

The goal is to develop good habits. It takes 21 or more consecutive days in order to form a habit.

You can start each challenge one at a time, start a few at a time or do them all at once.

Build each challenge seven consecutive days at a time until they all become routine

The guidelines for the seven day challenges are as follows:

- Answer the questions before beginning the challenge and after completing the challenge
- After completing seven consecutive days successfully, continue the challenge for seven more days
- Pay attention to the challenges that are difficult to complete or left incomplete.
- Jot down a few words in a journal on the difficulties for further exploration these are areas that will require more of our attention

5

Getting back to basics

A strong foundation ensures a strong structure.

My mother always told me common sense isn't always common.

This saying is all too real when it comes to losing weight. The belief that a pill, shake, or gadget can melt away pounds with little or no effort or personal responsibility is one of the reasons the diet industry is a billion dollar business.

With that being said, common sense would dictate that if you do things that cause you to gain weight, in order to lose weight, you have to stop doing those things.

Some of the simplest things we can do to improve our health and prevent unwanted weight gain are drinking water, getting the proper amount of sleep, and eating a well-balanced diet. These are basic components of weight loss that are often disregarded in favor of an unrealistic quick fix.

Water

H_2O is the most important weight loss formula on the market. Water is vital to our very survival since every bodily function depends upon it. Along with meeting our survival needs, water has many practical uses.

- Water is a great medicine. It helps relieve chronic fatigue, allergies, urinary tract infection, and it can decrease the risk of kidney stones and bladder cancer.

- Water helps relieve constipation and helps you to get regular. When you are not drinking enough water, the body takes it from your intestines, which can cause irregular bowel movements.

- Water is an appetite suppressant. Water reduces fat deposits allowing the liver to metabolize fat easier, and it makes you feel full so you will eat less.

- Water is the best solution for water retention. When your body is not getting enough water it holds on to every drop. This causes swollen feet, hands, and legs. When water is replenished regularly your body will release stored water.

- Water is great for your skin and hair. It moisturizes your skin by keeping it hydrated and younger looking. It also moisturizes your hair from the inside out.

- Water flushes out wastes in the body and improves muscle tone. Water keeps the body cool by maintaining normal body temperature in hot environments, as well as during exercise.

- Water aids in the digestion of food, delivers nutrients and hormones throughout the circulatory system, and cushions the joints.

Getting back to basics   41

Drinking enough water is extremely important. The human body is made up of at least 50-60% water; muscle is 72-75% water. Human beings can only survive, at most, a few days without it, because the cells and organs, cannot work without water.

The lack of water can result in dehydration, which causes headaches, fatigue, poor digestion, dizziness, sore joints and countless other problems that may be misinterpreted as more serious health issues. Loss of too much fluid can lead to seizures, coma, permanent brain damage, and even death. Severe dehydration (fluid loss of just 10% and up) is regarded as a medical emergency.

Dehydration can be caused by loss of water from diarrhea, vomiting, heavy sweating, diuretics, medications, caffeine, alcohol, as well as insufficient intake of water.

Symptoms of dehydration may include: thirst, dry mouth, dry eyes, infrequent urination, feeling lightheaded, frequent headaches, fatigue, and feeling sick to the stomach, dizzy or dazed.

By the time you feel thirsty, you are already dehydrated. That is why it is important to drink water regularly.

Your body may also signal to you that it is dehydrated by producing feelings that imitate hunger pangs.

If you notice that your urine is dark in color that is a sign that you need to drink more water. It is recommended that you drink at least eight 8oz glasses of water per day, or half of your body weight in ounces.

This does not include water consumed during workouts. Exercise and other physical demanding activities require more water than daily needs. The more physically demanding your exercise routine, the more fluid you lose.

- Be sure to stay hydrated and never wait until you are thirsty to drink water.
- Start your day by drinking a glass of water.
- Keep bottled water or a designated water glass on hand as a reminder to drink plenty of water.
- Drink water before meals.
- Make water your primary beverage of choice.
- Remember other beverages such as alcohol, energy drinks, or soft drinks actually aid in dehydration.

7 Day Water Challenge

Goal: to drink at least 64oz of water per day (eight 8oz glasses). Tap, bottled or filtered water. Water may be infused with fruit. **Do not use zero calorie water flavorings.**

Guidelines:

- Drink at least 8 ounces of water first thing in the morning
- Drink at least 8 ounces of water before meals and snacks
- Drink water before consuming other beverages
- Get a water bottle or glass to keep track of your water intake
- Record the ounces of water consumed each day of the seven days

Questions before starting challenge

1. How much water do I consume in a day?
2. What are my expectations going into this challenge?

Questions after completing 7 days

1. Did the challenge meet/exceed my expectations?
2. How do I feel after completing the first seven days?
3. What was the hardest part about this challenge?
4. Is this something I can do long term?
5. Changes I have noticed since completing the first seven days?

Sleep

Sleep is necessary for our nervous system to work properly. Too little sleep leaves us drowsy and unable to concentrate the next day. It also leads to impaired memory and physical performance.

Sleep gives neurons that are firing constantly while we are awake a chance to shut down and repair themselves.

Without sleep, neurons may become so depleted of energy or so polluted with by-products of normal cellular activities that they begin to malfunction. Continued sleep deprivation may lead to hallucinations and mood swings.

Cells in our body show increased production and reduced breakdown of proteins during deep sleep. Proteins are the building blocks needed for cell growth and for repair of damage from factors like stress. The body also repairs muscle tissue broken down by exercise during deep sleep.

Parts of the brain that control our emotions, decision-making processes, and social interactions show a drastic reduction in activity levels during deep sleep. This suggests that deep, restful sleep may help people maintain optimal emotional and social functioning while they are awake.

For most adults, seven to nine hours of sleep a night appears to be the best amount of sleep. Although some people may need as few as five hours or as many as ten hours of sleep each night.

Getting too little sleep creates a "sleep debt," which is much like being overdrawn at a bank. Eventually, your body will demand that the debt be repaid. For example, if you do not get enough sleep during the week, you may sleep half the day away on the weekends.

We do not adapt well to getting less sleep than we need. We may get used to being sleep-deprived, but our judgment, reaction time, patience, and other functions are still impaired.

To find out how much sleep you need, choose a day that you don't have to go to work or have any early morning appointments. Go to bed at your normal time the night before and turn off your alarm clock.

Let your body wake itself up naturally. Record how many hours from the time you went to sleep until the time you woke up and adjust your schedule to insure you get the right amount of sleep.

Getting a good night sleep is a very important component to leading a fit lifestyle. It is during sleep that our body can recharge, revive, and repair itself from emotional and physical stress.

Here are some tips on how to get good night sleep:

Set a schedule
Go to bed at a set time each night and get up at the same time each morning. "Sleeping in" on weekends makes it harder to wake up early on Monday morning because it resets your sleep cycles for a later awakening.

Exercise
Daily exercise often helps people sleep. Try to get your exercise about 5 to 6 hours before going to bed. If you exercise right before bedtime it may interfere with your ability to fall asleep.

Avoid caffeine, nicotine, and alcohol
Avoid drinks that contain caffeine, which can act as a stimulant. Sources of caffeine include coffee, chocolate, soft drinks, non-herbal teas, diet pills, and some pain relievers. Smokers tend to sleep very lightly and often wake up in the early morning due to nicotine withdrawal
Alcohol robs people of healthy deep sleep. There is a difference between passing out and deep restful sleep

Relax before bed
A warm bath, reading, or another relaxing routine can make it easier to fall sleep. You can train yourself to associate certain restful activities with sleep and make them part of your bedtime ritual.

Sleep until sunlight
If possible, wake up with the sun, or use very bright lights in the morning. Sunlight helps the body's internal biological clock reset itself each day.

Don't lie in bed awake
If you can't get to sleep, don't just lie in bed. Do something else, like reading, light stretching, or listening to music until you feel tired. The anxiety of being unable to fall asleep can actually contribute to insomnia.

Control your room temperature
Maintain a comfortable temperature in the bedroom. Extreme temperatures may disrupt sleep or prevent you from falling asleep.

If you have trouble falling asleep night after night, then you may have a sleep disorder and should see a physician.

7 Day Sleep Challenge

Goal: for the next seven days go to bed at the same time every night and wake up at the same time every morning.

Guidelines:
- Choose a bed time that will allow at least seven to nine hours of full sleep per night.
- Refrain from eating or drinking any beverages at least 2 hours before the set bed time.
- Make sure your bedroom is set up to support restful sleep
- Try not to fall asleep to music or the television
- If you naturally wake up before your alarm goes off, get up and re set the alarm to that time

Questions before starting the challenge
1. How much restful sleep do I get each night?
2. What, if anything, prevents me from getting a good night sleep?
3. Do I wake up feeling rested?

Questions after completing 7 days
1. How many hours of sleep per night do I need?
2. What changes have I noticed?
3. How do I feel after getting restful sleep?
4. Do I need an alarm clock to wake up?

Proper nutrition

How do you treat a body that is well hydrated and well rested? You provide it with a healthy variety of foods.

In our fast-paced society, it has become all too common to rely on fast food and microwave meals to feed ourselves and our families. Home cooked meals seem to only exist in childhood memories.

Super-sized portions are causing us to eat 150 more calories per day of high fat foods containing little or no nutritional value, so it is not hard to see why we are gaining weight.

Eating a well-balanced diet and making better food choices are major parts in overall weight loss and management.

One of the very best things we can do for our bodies and overall health is to adopt a plant based diet.

There are many benefits to adopting a plant based diet, some of which include:
- Lower cholesterol
- Lower saturated fats
- Increase in dietary fiber
- Decrease risk of colon, prostate and breast cancer
- Reverse type 2 diabetes
- Lowers risk of high blood pressure and hypertension
- Reduce arthritis symptoms

The list goes on and on. Studies also suggest that if you adopt a plant based diet at least twice a week, you can still reap the benefits.

Veganism

Veganism is the practice of abstaining from eating, using or purchasing foods and products that are made from animals, contain byproducts of animals, are tested on animals or exploit animals in any way. Such as: meat, dairy, clothing household items and beauty products.

Getting back to basics 49

When it comes to eating a plant based diet, the question many vegans get asked is, "How do you get your protein?" As shown on the *Choose my Vegan Plate* diagram, good sources of protein are contained in legumes and nuts. Dark green vegetables, such as broccoli, and grains like quinoa, contain as much protein as meat.

A healthy vegan plate should include:

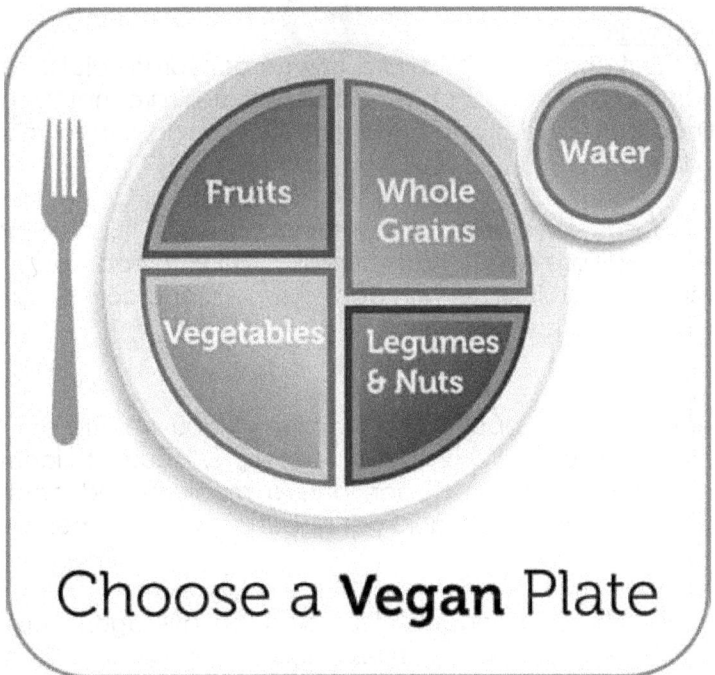

Source: choosemyplate.gov

Fruits: Fresh, frozen, dried, or vacuum sealed in juice, not syrup. Instead of high-fat, high-sugar deserts, put fruit on your plate.

Vegetables. Vary your mix of vegetables. Eat the rainbow and choose vegetables in colors like green, red, purple, yellow and orange.

Grains. Eat whole grains like brown rice, whole wheat bread, pasta, and oatmeal.

Protein. Choose beans, legumes, organic, non gmo tofu or tempeh, nuts dark green vegetables, and seeds.

Carbohydrates
With the trend leaning toward low-carbohydrate diets, it is important to know that all carbohydrates are not bad. Refined carbohydrates are the forms we should cut down in our diet.

Refined carbohydrates are contained in white flour, sugar, soft drinks, pre-sweetened cereals, white bread, pasta, crackers and fruit juices with added sugars, and corn syrups, just to name a few.

Fiber
Fiber helps with proper bowel function. If you were to eat 1 cup of bran cereal, 1/2 cup of carrots, 1/2 cup of kidney beans, a medium-sized pear, and a medium-sized apple together in 1 day, you would get about 30 grams of fiber.

Fats
No more than 30 percent of calories, on average, should come from fat per day, with less than 10 percent of calories from saturated fat

One of the easiest ways to cut down our fat intake is to ease up on sauces and condiments. Replace fat filled sandwich spreads with lower fat spreads like mustard. Try lower fat sauces on pasta like marinara instead of creamy sauces.

Do not drown an otherwise healthy salad with high-fat salad dressing. Always have your dressing on the side. Try squeezing lemon or lime on salads, the citrus really brings out the flavor of the vegetables.

Beware of low-fat and fat-free foods. Some contain high levels of sodium, sugars, and artificial ingredients that may cause adverse reactions in some people.

<u>Healthy fats</u>
Foods that contain healthy fats like omega three and omega six are considered good fats. The good fats you consume should come from nuts, coconut, grapeseed and olive oils, avocados and seeds like flax, hemp, or chia.

Food allergies
Some foods such as wheat and gluten can cause an allergic reaction in our bodies that can range from digestive issues, excess gas and bloating to more serious reactions such as celiac disease.
Some of us are allergic to nuts and break out in rashes and have trouble breathing if we consume them.

It is beneficial to get tested for food allergies or use the elimination diet and remove foods that are known allergens such as dairy, soy, wheat and nuts from your diet for a period of time then slowly reintroduce the foods one by one and see how your body reacts. If you have an adverse reaction after reintroducing a food then you know it should be permanently eliminated from your diet.

Becoming Vegan

I first adopted a vegan diet in 2010 after watching a documentary called *Eating*. I was a pescatarian (a vegetarian that eats fish and seafood) at the time and was intrigued by the vegan lifestyle and the health benefits of eliminating animal products from one's diet, like lower cholesterol, weight loss, lower risk for heart disease, diabetes, and cancer, all of which have plagued my family. My health issues at the time were self-induced. I was active in my alcoholism, and a pack and a half a day smoker, so I was hoping adopting a vegan diet would balance out some of the damage I was doing to myself.

I also liked the challenge of recreating my favorite foods without using animal products. I didn't transition into a vegan diet like it is suggested one should; I just got rid of all the meat and dairy products I had and jumped right in. I bought *The Complete Idiot's Guide to Vegan Cooking*, and I found a few websites that offered vegan recipes.

I did well for a few months. Then on Thanksgiving I was over my Mom's house; she had slaved all day cooking the traditional Thanksgiving feast, and I felt guilty about not eating it. I indulged that day and took a plate home and got back on track a few days after that. Christmas came, and I feasted then too.

Then on January 24th 2011, I decided to really do the best thing for my health and check myself into a detox facility and end my relationship with alcohol. Six months later, I quit smoking.

During this time, I was more focused on sobriety and decided giving into food cravings would be better than smoking or drinking so I ate any and everything. Over the next year I went from 168lbs to 220lbs. I was bigger than I had ever been in my life, and I started to experience edema, depression, low-energy, and insomnia.

In 2012 I, decided to try veganism again. This time, my reasoning for being vegan was more than health. I desired to live a more compassionate life and do my part to help the environment.

Now there are a few misconceptions to being vegan that I had to clear up this time around:

> Being vegan doesn't automatically mean you're healthy. There is just as much processed vegan food and junk food as there is processed food and junk food made with animal products. I decided I was going to eat a mostly clean vegan diet and not eat a lot of processed foods.
>
> There is a big misconception that vegans hate meat. I enjoy the taste of meat, but I don't enjoy the process of trying to digest it, the steroids, chemicals, the adrenaline, the antibiotics that are injected in the animals we eat, the blood, puss, and other bodily fluids, and the cruelty they endure just to wind up on our dinner plate. Plus the depletion of environmental resources that have to be used to run slaughter houses and chicken farms.
>
> Protein. The first question many vegans are asked is how do you get your protein? There is just as much if not more protein in dark green vegetables, soy, and seeds like chia or hemp seeds than there is in a piece of meat.
>
> I've been vegan for nine years now and I don't "look" like a vegan. This used to bother me, but I realize thin doesn't equal healthy. My blood pressure is excellent, my cholesterol is good and I don't have to rely on any medications. I am happy with the life choice I have made.

I am still learning about the vegan lifestyle and trying to incorporate it in every aspect of my life, not just my diet.

Portion Control

Along with making better food choices, we should also be conscious about our portions. The choose my vegan plate chart on page 49 gives you a visual idea of what portion sizes should look like.

Portion control is as important to weight loss as exercise. When starting on the road to change, pay attention to serving sizes on cereal, condiments, snack foods, nuts, oils, cooked pastas, salad dressings, and any other foods that are easy to overeat.

Once you have taken the time to measure and get an idea of what a proper portion size looks like, you will be able to measure your servings by sight.

Clean eating

Clean eating is eating food as close to its natural state as possible with little to no alteration. The basics to eating clean are as follows:

Eat lots of fresh fruits and vegetables – If fresh is not easily obtainable or economical, go for frozen. Avoid canned fruits and vegetable because they may contain high levels of salt and sugar and the canning process zaps out most of the foods nutritional value.

Choose baking, broiling, grilling, or steaming over frying in oils, coatings, and batters

Enjoy Grains - Stick to brown rice, quinoa, whole wheat and other whole grains.

Keep ingredients simple- Try not to purchase foods that have more than 3-6 ingredients in the ingredient list. If there are words in the ingredient list that can't be pronounced, err on the side of caution and don't eat it.

Remember, food is fuel for the body and the higher the quality and cleaner that fuel is, the more efficient our bodies will run.

More basics to consider:

Slow down and eat. By inhaling our meals, we miss out on the enjoyment of eating our food. We do not get a chance to savor the flavor or taste. Also, by eating food too fast, we often miss that feeling of being full and may overeat. Eating too quickly also causes stomach upset.

Make a habit of setting the fork down after each bite and chew our food thoroughly. When we feel satisfied (not stuffed), it is time to stop eating.

Schedule our meals; do not eat on the run. We tend to make poor food choices when eating on the go. Fast food and fattening snacks are usually the choices when we are in a rush. Setting aside time for meals and snacks gives us time to properly plan what we are going to eat.

Do not use time set aside for meals for shopping and errands. Doing so may mean that we tend to eat more to make up for it later in the evening.

Eat at the table, not in front of the TV. If we have a family, eating meals at the table is one of the most basic and satisfying bonding rituals there is. Eating at the table also helps us to concentrate on what we are putting in our mouths and we enjoy our food more.

7 Day portion control & clean vegan eating challenge

Goal: for the next seven days prepare at least one meal per day using the portion size guidelines on the choose my plate chart and make the meal clean and vegan.

Portion control:
- Pay attention to the serving sizes noted in the nutritional information section of drinks and packaged foods
- Use a plate or containers that are already labeled with portion sizes to help you plan your meals.

Clean eating:
- Replace meat in one meal with a vegetable based protein like beans, legumes, tofu or a dark leafy vegetable
- Eat vegetables plain; try using herbs and low salt flavorings for seasoning
- Do not coat food in flour or breading
- No dairy or cheese
- Keep food as close to its original form as possible

Questions before challenge:
1. What are my expectations going into this challenge?
2. What parts of this challenge are going to be difficult for me?
3. Are my current portion sizes more/less than what is depicted on the choose my plate chart?
4. What sauces and condiments do I use the most?
5. How often do I eat fried/battered foods?

Questions after completing 7 days:
1. How do I feel after the first 7 days of this challenge?
2. What was the hardest part of the first seven days?
3. What changes, if any, have I noticed?
4. How does eating clean vegan compare to my normal way of eating?
5. Is this something I can do long term?

58   I Know How to Lose Weight, So Why Haven't I?

6

Get moving

When starting an exercise program, remember some is better than none.

Do we spend most of our day in motion or motionless? When was the last time we participated in regular physical activity?

Most of us sit at a desk, sit in the car, sit at the kitchen table or sit on the couch. Add up all of that sitting, and we have spent most of our days and our evenings motionless. Physical inactivity can contribute to unwanted weight gain, poor blood circulation, stiff joints, and chronic fatigue.

Regular physical activity can:
- Help keep weight at healthy levels
- Reduce the risks of some cancers
- Lower the risks of cardiovascular disease
- Strengthen bones and muscle
- Improve mood and mental health

Regular physical exercise has more benefits than just weight loss. So even if losing weight is not our primary goal, increasing our physical activity can be beneficial.

Posture

Before committing to being more physically active we should learn the basics of body alignment. In order to learn how to use our bodies in a more efficient manner we should first focus on our posture.

Posture is the position in which we hold our bodies upright against gravity while standing, sitting or lying down.

Good posture involves training our bodies to stand, walk, sit and lie in positions where the least strain is placed on supporting muscles and ligaments during movement or weight-bearing activities.

Proper posture keeps joints and bones in the proper alignment, prevents wear and tear of joints which can lead to arthritis, fatigue, lower back pain and muscle strain.

Excess weight gain, pregnancy, high-heeled shoes, weak muscles and poor body mechanics contribute to poor posture.

Maintaining proper position during movement is considered as having good body mechanics. Improving our body mechanics means becoming aware of our body position during all activities.

Practice using these techniques for standing sitting, driving, and sleeping to help improve our posture.

Correct standing position
- Hold your head up straight with your chin in. Do not tilt your head forward, backward or sideways.
- Make sure your earlobes are in line with the middle of your shoulders.
- Keep your shoulder blades back.
- Keep your chest forward.
- Keep your knees straight.
- Stretch the top of your head toward the ceiling.

Get moving   61

- Tuck your stomach in. Do not tilt your pelvis forward or backward.
- The arches in your feet should be supported.
- Avoid standing in the same position for a long time.

Correct sitting position.
- Sit up with your back straight and your shoulders back. Your buttocks should touch the back of your chair. All three normal back curves should be present while sitting.
- A small, rolled-up towel or a lumbar roll can be used to help you maintain the normal curves in your back.
- Distribute your body weight evenly on both hips. Bend your knees at a right angle. Keep your knees even with or slightly higher than your hips (use a foot rest or stool if necessary). Your legs should not be crossed.
- Keep your feet flat on the floor.
- Try to avoid sitting in the same position for more than 30 minutes.
- At work, adjust your chair height and work station so you can sit up close to your work area and tilt your keyboard (if you use one) up toward you. Rest your elbows and arms on your chair or desk, keeping your shoulders relaxed.
- When sitting in a chair that rolls and pivots, don't twist at the waist while sitting. Instead, turn your whole body.
- When standing up from the sitting position, move to the front of the seat of your chair. Stand up by straightening your legs. Avoid bending forward at your waist.
- When driving, use a back support (lumbar roll) at the curve of your back. Your knees should be at the same level or higher than your hips.
- Move the seat close to the steering wheel to support the curve of your back. The seat should be close enough to allow your knees to bend and your feet to reach the pedals.

Correct sleeping position
- No matter what position you lie in, the pillow should be under your head, but not your shoulders. The pillow should be a thickness that allows your head to be in a normal position.
- Try to sleep in a position which helps you maintain the curve in your back (such as on your back with a pillow under your knees, a lumbar roll under your lower back, or on your side with your knees slightly bent).
- Do not sleep on your side with your knees drawn up to your chest.
- You may want to avoid sleeping on your stomach, especially on a saggy mattress, since this can cause back strain and can be uncomfortable for your neck.
- Select a firm mattress and box spring set that does not sag. If necessary, place a board under your mattress. You can also place the mattress on the floor temporarily if necessary. If you've always slept on a soft surface, it may be more painful to change to a hard surface. Try to do what's most comfortable for you.
- Try using a back support (lumbar support) at night to make you more comfortable. A rolled sheet or towel tied around your waist may be helpful.
- When standing up from the lying position, turn on your side; draw up both knees, and swing your legs on the side of the bed. Sit up by pushing yourself up with your hands. Avoid bending forward at your waist.

What does posture have to do with exercise and weight loss we may ask - a lot. The importance of proper posture is often overlooked as a key component of fitness. Poor posture can lead to injury when performing certain exercises, and proper posture can increase the efficiency of exercises for better results. Working on our posture alone can give our bodies a better appearance. Our muscles will tighten in core areas such as our lower back, abdominal and pelvic muscles. Our bodies will appear to be in better proportion.

Learning proper posture and body mechanics helps make the transition from sedentary to active more effective. Once we master how to move properly, we can concentrate on the type of movement to perform.

Yoga is a good way to improve posture. Basic yoga poses focus on core muscles and proper body alignment.

Exercise
Starting any fitness program can be difficult. Most of us view exercise as a chore. When we do commit to a regular exercise routine, we sometimes try to do too much too soon and end up quitting.

When beginning to add exercise to our healthy lifestyle plan, remember these important factors:

- Moving too far ahead in activity level can expose us to serious injury.
- When we start at the top of the workout level, we have nowhere else to go. If we hit a point of stagnation before reaching our fitness goal, we have to increase our activity, which is already too high to begin with, in order to continue progressing.
- Working out too hard too soon takes a lot out of us physically and mentally. Face it - if we know we have to work out extra hard to lose weight, it is extremely difficult to get motivated to do it.

- We can't out train a bad diet. If we are still eating high fat high calorie highly processed foods, no amount of exercise will get us to our goal.

Walking is one of the easiest and most effective forms of exercise. Walking is something most of us do every day in one form or another. Walking is low impact and easy on the joints. It is easier to make a workout of walking than it is to go to a gym or start any other workout routine.
If we choose walking as our introduction into getting more physical activity, incorporate some of these ideas into our daily routine.

- Take a 10-minute stroll down the block and back. Or, buy a motorized treadmill, and use it while we're watching our favorite shows.
- Wake up 15 minutes earlier than usual, and squeeze in a quick stroll before our morning coffee.
- Look for moments during the day when we're walking anyway and extend our walk into a mini-workout.

Physical activity should be approached in stages.
Going from little or no activity to an hour and a half per day of exercise is a sure way to burn ourselves out or risk injury.

That is why it is important to start at a beginning activity level and work our way up.

Choose activities or hobbies that involve movement.

- Take a dance or self-defense class or become a mall walker (as long as you stay away from the food court).
- Yoga is a great way to get into regular exercise. Yoga loosens joints, improves range of motion in joints, lowers blood pressure, focuses on proper breathing, and increases flexibility.
- Sports are a good way to have fun and get active. Bowling, golf, basketball, softball, soccer are just a few.

Everyone is different. Some exercises work better for some people than for other people.

Before starting any exercise program, consult your physician.

The key to incorporating exercise in our healthy lifestyle plan is to get rid of all the excuses.

Excuse #1: I do not have enough time to exercise.

We can all squeeze out 5 minutes a day. Some is better than none. If we do not miss an episode of our favorite TV show, then there is our time right there. Record the show, and get in a workout, or workout while watching it.

The truth is, we choose not to spend some of our free time exercising. The psychology is simple: We make time for what we enjoy, and we put off - or avoid entirely - what we don't.

Excuse #2: I am too tired to exercise.

We may need more sleep, or we may be procrastinating. If we are truly committed to change, we have to fight the urge to procrastinate and just do it. Exercising will make us feel less tired. The endorphins released after a workout will lift our spirits and make us glad we did not give up.
Do something! Run in place or take a short walk if we do not feel like doing a full workout.

Make sure we are not working out too hard. If we are jumping too far ahead in activity level, constant fatigue is a sure sign to decrease intensity.

Excuse #3: I wasn't in the mood.

Tough it out in the early weeks, and keep reminding ourselves that it will get easier. Research shows that people who exercised steadily for three months fell into the habit and were less likely to quit. Mix up our routine to prevent boredom with our workouts. Remind ourselves why we need exercise - to improve our overall physical and mental wellbeing.

Excuse #4: I cannot work out alone.

There **is** strength in numbers, but one person can make a difference. Getting motivated to start an exercise program is difficult enough; having to do it alone can make getting started harder for some.

Having a workout buddy can help us stay motivated if they are as committed to change as we are. If not, they can do more harm than good. The key is to find a reliable, motivated partner with whom to workout. A close friend, family member or a workout club are good ways to find workout buddies.

If all else fails, get a workout DVD, stream a workout on your favorite streaming service and bond with the friendly faces onscreen.

There are some positives to working out alone. It gives us time to meditate. We do not have to try and hold a conversation while breathing heavily. We do not have to be embarrassed about how much we are sweating, and we do not have to try and kill ourselves in order to keep up with our partner.

The key is to get rid of the excuses and find ways to make exercise less of a *chore* and more of a *choice*.

- *Make it fun.* If we don't love exercise, try to bring things we do love into the exercise experience. Watch TV, listen to music, or chat with a friend during our workout.
- *Make it convenient.* If we want exercise to become a habit, make it fit easily into our schedule. A few short exercise sessions a day are as valuable as one extended session.
- *Be realistic.* Expect at least a couple of weeks to go by before we start to notice any changes in our bodies.
- *Be flexible.* With work and family life tugging at us, it's easy to get bumped from our exercise routine. Do not give up. Anticipate some unexpected interruptions. If we work out Monday, Wednesday, and Friday and for some reason we could not get Monday's workout in, do it on Tuesday. Do not get so hung up on schedules that we do not get our workout in.
- *Ask ourselves three simple questions:* Do I look forward to this? Do I enjoy doing it? Do I feel good afterward? If we can honestly answer yes to one or more questions, we will be more likely to stick with it.

Here are more ways to make exercise a healthy and safe habit:

- Start to exercise slowly and add more exercise over time. If we feel our current exercise routine is no longer challenging, then we know it is time to increase the intensity.
- Set exercise goals for ourselves. For instance, challenge ourselves to get through an exercise routine without stopping or focus on proper form.
- Pay attention to our bodies. Some soreness or stiffness is okay when we first start exercising. If we have pain, stop the exercise. We may have pulled a muscle or hurt a joint.
- Take the time to warm up before we exercise and cool down after we exercise.

- Wear comfortable clothing that is right for the weather.
- Exercise in a safe place.
- Get exercise at least three days a week. Make exercise a habit. Remember some is always better than none.
- Enjoy how we feel after exercising.
- Don't give up if we miss a few days of exercise. We can start again.
- Stop exercising right away if we feel dizzy or nauseous, experience pain in our upper bodies, have cold sweats, get pale, or faint.

7 Day walking challenge

Goal: jump start physical activity by including more walking in your day.

Include more walking by:
- Parking further from entrances
- Take a walk around the block
- Walk a couple of laps around the grocery store before shopping
- Take a five minute walk before lunch
- If you own a treadmill, walk on it for 5 minutes

Questions prior to starting challenge:
1. When can I get in a walk during the day?
2. What are my expectations for this challenge?

Questions after completing seven days:
1. How much walking did I get in per day?
2. How do I feel after completing seven days?
3. Is this something I can do long term?

7

Love ourselves now

I am a work in progress, I am not in a race, I move in my own time, and at my own pace.

One concept that would seem to be a no-brainier is the concept of self-love. Realistically, out of all the times we say the words, "I love you," how many times do we say it to ourselves?

When it comes to losing weight and adopting a healthier lifestyle, love is the last thing we show ourselves when the inner critic starts to belittle and berate us.

Love is patient; love is kind; love is compassionate. Change does not happen until we love who we are now, and out of that love better choices and behaviors can be nurtured.
If we love ourselves now, we would realize weight loss is not a magic fix-all; losing 20lbs is not going to solve all of our problems.

I hear it (and say it) all the time:

"I'm not buying new clothes until I lose some weight."
"If I wasn't so fat, maybe I would go out."

"When I lose this weight, then I'll be..."
   "Better"
   "Happier"
   "Prettier"
   "More successful"
These are not phrases we would say to a loved one, so why say them to ourselves?

Self-love
Self-love is the act of having appreciation for oneself that *grows from actions* that support our physical, psychological and spiritual growth. Taking care of our health, taking time to de-stress, and staying connected to our higher power are all ways of showing self-love. Know our own worth and understand that we are the most important person in our lives.

Self-compassion
Self-compassion is the ability to show ourselves kindness and forgiveness when we feel like we have failed, feel inadequate or feel pain. Recognizing our humanity and showing ourselves patience are steps toward self-compassion.

Self-esteem
Self-esteem is our overall sense of self-worth and personal value.

Body Image
Body image is defined as how we feel about our beauty and sexual attractiveness of our own bodies. Oftentimes, if we don't look like the airbrushed models in the magazines or the Botox-filled reality stars on TV, or photoshopped Instagram models, we tend to have a low body image.

Learning to be comfortable with the body we are in now will help to relieve a lot of the pressure and unrealistic expectations we put on ourselves and will prevent us from falling into the quick-fix mentality.

What we feel on the inside shows on the outside. If we feel down, depressed and unworthy, we tend to slouch, avoid eye contact and look tired.

If we feel like no matter what, we are worthy, we smile more and people are drawn to our positive energy.

There are many women who go through dramatic changes on the outside, but still carry the same self-concept on the inside. It is just as important to *think* like the person we want to be as it is to *look* like the person we want to be.

Building confidence
Building our confidence is one way to improve our self-esteem. Taking small risks, acknowledging accomplishments and fulfilling our dreams are confidence boosters.

Being brave enough to take a chance or try something new will have us feeling stronger and more capable. It is never too late to build confidence in ourselves.

By staying stagnant for the sake of doing the "right thing" or for familiarity, we allow our fears to get the best of us and lessen the quality of our lives.

If there is a major change we want to make in our lives, think it through and ask ourselves, "What is the worst thing that can happen?" Create a scenario of what may happen and how we would handle it. Thinking a situation through and planning for the worst takes away the anxiety and gives us the strength to go for it.

Be more self-ish
This doesn't mean don't be kind to others; this just means take care of ourselves first. Make sure our needs are met. Being a people-pleaser and a doormat essentially gives others the power over our self-worth.

Don't be available to everyone who asks something from us, even people close to us. We may end up spending less time on our own concerns and wind up harboring resentments.

We may find ourselves free of a lot of phony friends and users. Relationships with true friends and loved ones will grow stronger as we grow stronger.

Stay true to ourselves and our feelings.
Stop worrying about what people think. When we let the opinions of others mold our thoughts and feelings about ourselves, we relinquish our power.

Do what is right for us. After all, we are the ones who have to live with our decisions.

Pay attention to our bodies; acknowledge the feelings of discomfort our bodies give us when things don't "feel" right.

Check in with ourselves regularly. Get to a point where we know when our bodies need something.

Loving who we are right now, in this moment, can make all of the difference in the world. Make sure to tell ourselves, "I love you" everyday.

7 Day Love ourselves challenge

Goal: reverse negative self-talk by affirming ourselves

Guidelines:
- Start each day by expressing love for a part of our bodies or a trait we like about ourselves "I love my nose" " I love that I can draw".
- Give ourselves compliments throughout the day
- Do not criticize ourselves and immediately stop negative self talk

Questions before starting challenge:
1. How often do I criticize myself daily?
2. How often do I complement myself daily?
3. What are my expectations for this challenge?

Questions after completing challenge:
1. How did it feel showing love towards myself? Was it hard to come up with things to love? Did it get easier?
2. What changes, if any, have I noticed in the way I talk to myself?

76 I Know How to Lose Weight, So Why Haven't I?

So *Why* Haven't I?

I Know How to Lose Weight, So Why Haven't I?

8

What's really going on?

You won't know where you are going if you don't know where you are.

Ok, so we know how this works, eat right, get plenty of water, rest, and exercise - but knowing is half the battle. The other half of the battle may be what we are feeling.

Emotions play a role in how we approach lifestyle change. Thoughts, beliefs, and how we react to our environment can silently and subconsciously derail our best efforts.

Taking time to address how we feel can give us better insight on why sustaining a healthy lifestyle may be eluding us.

How did I get here?
When was the last time we considered ourselves to be fit? Think back on how life was like then.
- Were we active?
- Did we participate in sports?
- Or were we one of those people that could eat anything and not gain weight?

Once we find our place in time, think of all of the changes that have taken place from that point until now and how they may have contributed to our current weight gain.
- Has it taken months or years to get us to our current weight?
- How many times did we diet during that time period?

Now take the time to address where we are in the moment.
- What does living a healthy lifestyle look like, feel like?
- What expectations do we have around being healthy?
- How will being healthier improve our life?
- What will it take to maintain a healthy lifestyle?
- What are we willing to do?

Why we eat/Emotional factors

What do we use food for? Why do we eat? "Because I'm hungry," we may be thinking. That is the obvious answer, but many of us eat for reasons other than hunger and nourishment.

Some of us eat based on emotions and not on physical needs. If we used food for its intended purpose, many of us wouldn't have problems with our weight.

When we eat based on emotions, it has nothing to do with hunger. Once we are aware of this, we can better plan our strategy to handle emotional eating.

When we eat to fulfill emotional needs, we usually eat junk food or comfort foods that give us warm fuzzy feelings as we are consuming them, but immediately leave us feeling unfulfilled. Then the emotion that triggered the urge to eat is still there. Some of the emotional triggers are:

- Anger - at ourselves, someone else, or a situation. Food is used to suppress our feelings instead of releasing them. A better solution would be to write out our feelings and find a way to express them to the person we were angry with in the most constructive way possible. If we are not able to talk with the person that made us angry writing our feelings down is at least a positive way to release emotions instead of eating.

- Hopelessness - when we feel like nothing matters, nothing is going right and nothing is going to change. We express these feelings by raiding the fridge. This often leads to self-loathing because we can't believe we ate so much. A better solution would be to think of those less fortunate than us. There are people without food, freedom, rights or homes. Scream if we feel like screaming, cry if we feel like crying, call a friend and vent, but let it out, let it go and don't try to heal it with food.

- Lack of control - feeling like everything and everyone has control over us, but us. The only thing we can control is food. A better solution is to realize we have control over the choices we make, and we choose to give up control to people in our lives. We place ourselves in the control of others when we are eager to please and when we put their needs before our own. Learn to say no and put ourselves first.

- Feeling unappreciated – With this trigger when accomplishments go unnoticed we tend to reward ourselves with food to compensate. A better solution is self-recognition. Give ourselves a certificate of accomplishment. Toot our own horn; tell others of our accomplishments. Sometimes we do not get recognition from others because they are not aware of what we have achieved. Keep a scrapbook or journal. Remember, the satisfaction we get from accomplishing a goal is reward enough.

- Boredom - Feeling lonely and like there is nothing to do. No one to call. Nowhere to go. Nothing but food and opportunity. A better solution would be to go for a walk, take up a hobby, housework or read a book. Make a list of things we like to do or need to do, so when boredom hits, we can fill the time and not your waistline.

Refer to the chart on the next page to find new coping mechanisms for emotional triggers.

Feeing	Old behavior	New behavior
Anger	Eating to suppress emotions	Write a letter to release anger
Hopelessness	Binge eating	Focus on gratitude. Do something for someone less fortunate
Lack of control	Poor food choices	Replace poor food choices with better ones
Feeling unappreciated	Use food as a reward	Reward yourself in other ways
Boredom	Eating to pass time	Find a hobby

Stress

Stress is probably the most common and potentially life-threatening of states. It is described as a feeling of both emotional and/or physical tension.

When situations are viewed to be difficult or unbearable, emotional stress usually occurs. Physical stress often causes emotional stress, and emotional stress can manifest as physical upset such as headaches or stomach discomfort.

Stress is a major roadblock to change. Stress can come from all facets of our lives. How we cope with stress has a bearing on our overall well-being.

Look at all of the stressors we may face:
Job
- performance
- deadlines
- daily tasks,

Family
- schedules
- children
- relationships

Physical
- health
- illness
- daily activities

Responsibilities
- bills
- home
- obligations

Expectations
- of ourselves
- from others
- from society

Make a list of these stressors. How many are self- induced? Demands and unrealistic expectations we place on ourselves, trying to please everyone, and trying to be perfect can cause undue stress.

How many stressors are over things that are beyond our control, worrying about what others think of us, if they think of us, the weather, war, and global warming? These are things that many of us worry about. As significant as some things are, we have no control over what people think or what they may or may not do, so it does us no good to get stressed out over them.

Cross out the ones that are beyond our control and develop a plan to reduce and eliminate the self-induced stressors. We are devoting useful energy to useless worries.

Learning to relieve stress involves making changes physically and emotionally. Changes in our attitudes can minimize the effects of stress. Positive thinking, staying away from negative people, situations and refocusing negative thoughts, can help minimize stress. Having fun and taking a break when things get overwhelming can keep a situation from getting too stressful.

Meditate. Take a few minutes a day to focus on positive thoughts and tap into positive energy within. Breathe deeply inhaling through our noses taking a small pause and exhaling through our mouths. Slowly allow all negative thoughts and feelings to flow out of our bodies with each cleansing breath.

Relax. Take a hot bath with candles and soothing fragrances.

Be creative. Tap into those creative resources and make something that is truly a reflection of us.

> I draw and write poetry when I am upset or stressed. I feel much better after creating my own little work of art. Being creative is a positive outlet for negative emotions.

Depression

Depression is a mental state that manifests in feelings of hopelessness and despair. Many factors contribute to depression. As we begin to change from childhood to adolescence, the hormonal changes that take place in our bodies also have an emotional effect.

Forming an identity, awareness of sexuality, increased responsibility and expectations are all stressors that can contribute to depression as early as teenage years.

Depression can have a profound effect on our lives as well as our weight.

Feelings brought on by depression affect us in a way that prevents us from feeling worthy. Feelings such as these may lead to self-medication in the form of emotional eating or even alcohol and drug abuse.

Recognition and acknowledgement of these feelings is the first step to overcoming them.

Getting help is the second step. The stigma of seeking counseling is slowly fading as mental health and prevention are gaining more attention.

It is better to get treated for mental illness than to have it ruin our quality of life. For more information on depression and other mental health issues visit:
http://www.mentalhealth.gov/

I am still dealing with depression. I remember days when I felt so hopeless that I would not get out of bed. When I did get up, I was on autopilot doing just what I had to do for myself. I had no energy. I did not want to do anything or go anywhere.

Escaping out of my emotional prison takes affirmations, positive thinking and seeking professional counseling.

I try not to allow myself to succumb to feelings of hopelessness. Whether I feel like it or not, I get myself out of bed. I keep positive messages and affirmations close at hand to give myself an emotional pick me up. I eat more fresh fruits and vegetables and avoid overly processed foods. I take walks, meditate or do light exercise.

I write my feelings down in a journal as a way to release them. Once they are written down in the journal I have to leave those feelings there.

I keep regular appointments with a therapist, even when I am feeling good. It helps me to learn better ways to cope with my bouts of depression and in most cases, avoid having them.

Procrastination

Getting started on any change in lifestyle is the hardest thing to do, especially if we procrastinate. I, personally, think I have procrastination down to an art form. As helpful as I want this book to be, the act of writing it is actually avoidance of starting my own lifestyle change.

Putting things off just gives us more things to deal with later. Procrastination is an excuse to avoid things we know we need and want to do. It is really not a good coping tool.

As I mentioned, procrastination refers to the avoidance of a specific task or goal that needs to be accomplished. The emotions triggered by procrastination include guilt, laziness, self-consciousness and anxiety. Procrastination also implies that if we procrastinate, we are bad and lack worth as a person.

In order to get past the procrastination roadblock, we must take a hard look at situations where we have goals or work that is not being completed.

Is it poor time management? Or do we know how to make time for other things and other people, but not for the things we need to accomplish? Then, procrastination may be an avoidance tool for us. Many individuals use the following reasons for avoiding tasks:

Lack of relevance
If something is neither relevant nor meaningful to us personally, it may be difficult to get motivated even to begin.

Lack of interest
If a goal is not of interest to us, we may be reluctant to spend the necessary time to see it to conclusion.

Perfectionism
Having unreachable standards will discourage us from pursuing a task. For example, waiting for the perfect time,

condition, and set of circumstances to start working on losing weight will have us waiting forever. Remember, there is no such thing as perfection.

Evaluation anxiety
Since others' responses to our progress are not within our control, we may become anxious worrying what others think.

Ambiguity
If we are uncertain of what we want to accomplish as far as weight loss and fitness goals, it may be difficult to get started.

Apprehension
If we are trying a different approach to what has been ingrained in our psyche concerning weight loss and we do not know what the outcome will be, the uncertainty may inhibit our desire to begin.

Inability to handle the task
Lack of understanding, support or motivation, may make us feel that we lack the personal resources to reach our goal and we may avoid it completely.

Fear of success or failure
Although success and failure are at different ends of the accomplishment scale, both come with their own set of emotions. Failure can affect our self esteem and worth. Success can affect how we foresee new expectations and responsibilities as a result of success. Fear of either can cause us to avoid a goal.

Once we have overcome the emotional block by acknowledging our procrastination (i.e. guilt, anxiety, and feelings of inadequacy), we need to clearly specify how we procrastinate.

Consider the following:

- Do we act as though if we ignore a task, it will go away?
- Do we underestimate the work involved in the task? Like setting unrealistic weight loss goals, like losing in two weeks the 40lbs it took us a year to gain?
- Do we deceive ourselves into believing that a lesser standard is acceptable? Like switching to diet soda and baked chips for a late night snack is a sufficient change in eating habits?
- Do we deceive ourselves by substituting one worthy activity for another? We call our girlfriend when we are supposed to be working out. She has a problem so we provide her with a shoulder to cry on. It is good to be there for a friend, but if we are making phone calls instead of working out at the time we have set aside for exercise, you are procrastinating.
- Do we believe that repeated delays are harmless? It's time for our after dinner walk, but we start washing dishes. We re-arrange the refrigerator and plan our meals for the month, or balance our checkbook. Anything to avoid the task at hand.
- Do we dramatize a commitment to a task rather than actually doing it? An example is buying new workout DVD's and clothing, or turning down brunch with the girls, but still not exercising as planned. We keep ourselves in a constant state of unproductive readiness to exercise without ever getting started.
- Do we persevere on only one portion of the task? We revise and re-revise our daily schedule, but don't deal with other components like planning meals, and activities. The schedule is important, but not at the expense of the entire plan.
- Do we become paralyzed in deciding between alternative choices? Spending too much time deciding between working out at home or joining a gym that we do not take any action.

- Do we write a book about road blocks to starting a healthy lifestyle change to avoid starting a healthy lifestyle change.

If we can recognize ourselves in any of these scenarios, we may be ready to change this behavior pattern. These steps may help us deal with our procrastination.

Make honest decisions about our goals. Admit to ourselves if we only want to spend minimal amount of effort or time on a particular task; do not allow feelings of guilt to interfere.
Examine the consequences of our investment to reaching our goals. What we put in to achieving the goal will determine how soon we will reach it and how close we will come to achieving the desired result.

If we wait until the last minute, like the month before the goal we set was supposed to be reached, we place ourselves under pressure to achieve the goal in an unrealistic timeframe. The fact that we recognize the goal is unachievable in the time we have will give us an excuse to procrastinate.

Give ourselves time to reach our goal which may include those times when we veer from the plan. Given enough time, we can correct our mistakes and move forward without the added anxiety.

Break the goal down into segments. Do not fool ourselves by believing we can do more than is realistically possible.
Know when to take time to step back from a task and relax before letting it overwhelm us.

Keep track of our progress. Be aware of the pitfalls discussed earlier. Plan a strategy to handle problems when they arise and do something about them quickly.

Try starting a task and setting a timer for ten minutes. Give ourselves permission to stop the task after the ten minute alarm goes off. More than likely we will not want to stop working on the task once we have been doing it for ten minutes.

Be reasonable in our expectations of ourselves. Perfection or extremely strict expectations may cause us to rebel and sabotage our progress.

Summed up - procrastination is a byproduct of fear. We put things off out of fear. Fear can motivate us to accomplish goals as well as motivate us to avoid them. Remember putting off tomorrow what one can do today leaves more to do tomorrow.

Changing seasons
I've worked in an office with women of all shapes, sizes, races, ethnicities, religious backgrounds, and ages. As diverse as our lives and experiences were, there was one common thread we all shared - the war with weight.

It seemed our attitudes and dress sizes changed like the seasons. In the winter, we were feeding each other with complaints and comfort foods.

In the spring, the office was full of water bottles diet shakes, pills and e-mail forwards of the newest diet craze. Complaints turned into encouragements, diet clubs and lunchtime workouts were created.
Those who were successful became the topic of office gossip; those that were unsuccessful became the gossipers.

Summer brought smiles, sandals and salads. Spirits were higher and weights were lower.

Come fall, the diet buzz died down, the lunchtime workouts were replaced by lunch and the comfort foods found their way back. By winter, the "feast" was in full swing.

The success stories were back to their pre-diet weight plus a few extra pounds.

In all seriousness, seasonal changes can have an effect on our mood and motivation. It has been documented that the absence of sunlight during winter months in areas that experience all four seasons, makes many people feel less energetic and more moody. In some cases it can develop into a form of clinical depression known as seasonal affective disorder

Symptoms of seasonal affective disorder may include:

- Irritability
- Tiredness or low-energy
- Problems getting along with other people
- Hypersensitivity to rejection
- Heavy, "leaden" feeling in the arms or legs
- Oversleeping
- Appetite changes, especially a craving for foods high in carbohydrates
- Weight gain

Trauma
Trauma is defined as a deeply distressing or disturbing experience. There is a link between weight gain and trauma, which would suggest that it could be more than a poor diet and lack of exercise making it difficult to lose weight.

Trauma can create an increase of hormones in the body that can cause weight gain. Trauma also has an effect on the nervous system. When a traumatic event happens that the conscious mind cannot handle and our fight or flight response is compromised, our bodies take over and create a barrier of protection against further trauma.

Psychologically weight gain represents unresolved or unaddressed emotions we have held in our bodies as a result of traumatic experiences such as sexual abuse or emotional trauma.

To overcome the physical effects of trauma takes addressing emotions and feelings that can be uncomfortable to deal with. Seek a safe environment, a support group or professional help to assist us in this process.

Start with self-forgiveness for any guilt, shame or blame we may have toward ourselves. Affirm our worth and thank our bodies for taking care of us.

> I was in an abusive relationship for almost three years.
>
> Over the course of that relationship I went from 160 to 203lbs. It was odd because during that time, I wasn't over eating and I was physically active. It seemed the more fearful I became, the more weight I put on.
>
> For years after the relationship ended, I stayed on auto pilot afraid to admit to myself how much that relationship affected me.
>
> I withdrew from social situations, and any attention I would receive from men would make me extremely anxious and filled with fear.
>
> It wasn't until early 2015 that I really started to deal with what had happened to me and how it has affected my self-image, self-worth, self-esteem and weight.
>
> To this day I still struggle to get my weight at a healthy level.
>
> I realize I have to get rid of the emotional weight of being abused so I can let go of the physical weight.

9

Mind Games

You are who you think you are

Mind games are the thoughts we have that play with our self-image, self-esteem and self-worth. Those scenarios we play out in our heads based on our deepest fears and negative experiences. Those thoughts that keep us stuck in bad habits and cause anxiety when presented with change. The beliefs that cause us to make excuses and build resistance toward the very thing we want to accomplish. Those justifications we make for irrational behavior and decision-making.

Self-sabotage

> I am getting close to my goal, and I start to see significant changes. Then, all of a sudden I think to myself, "What if this perfect existence I have created in my head doesn't come to pass once I reach my goal?" I will be the same person with the same problems, just thinner. Then I find myself, sleeping in, skipping workouts and binge eating as a result.

One of the most detrimental mind games we play on ourselves is self sabotage. Self-sabotage is a mind game that triggers behaviors we display when we try to save ourselves from our own negative emotions. Instead of facing our fears and dealing with our hurts, we get in our own way to prevent ourselves from dealing with those emotions.

When we sabotage ourselves, we create situations in our minds based on the worst case scenario. That one bad day we have in our weight loss journey becomes, "I wasn't going to lose weight anyway so there is no use in fooling myself that I had a chance." Then, the one day turns into several days, then weeks, months, and so on. Or we set unrealistic goals and expectations for ourselves. Or just when we get close to reaching our goal anxiety sets in, and we begin to do things that derail our efforts.

The fear of failure is most times seen as the motivating force behind self-sabotage, but fear of success can also cause uneasiness. Unknown expectations and responsibilities associated with success can lead us to give in to behaviors that will prevent us from having to deal with that reality.

If we find ourselves displaying these behaviors, we may be guilty of self-sabotage.

Focusing on what is not working or not right
Thinking about what is going wrong can have us feeling dissatisfied and can lower our motivation and ambition. Pay attention to how often we speak about things that aren't working. Instead ask ourselves, "What's going right?" Start to notice all the things, no matter how small, that are working well. Make a list of all the things that are working and be grateful for those things instead of focusing on what is not right.

Fear
Worrying too much about the future and what is going to happen or might happen can keep us paralyzed and afraid to take action. Focus on the present. We can't control or

predict the future, and we don't have control over other people's behavior. All we have is today, and the only person we can control is ourselves. Stay in the moment, and don't worry about things that are beyond our control.

Feeling you have no value.
Do we often criticize ourselves or struggle to accept compliments? Do we forget about all our accomplishment and only focus on our mistakes? Lacking self-worth means we aren't allowing ourselves to love ourselves.

Turn off the negative self talk. When we hear that inner critic, shut if off immediately. Acknowledge all of our accomplishments, even the small ones. Keep a list of all the things we have done well throughout the day. Compliment ourselves on something we did that we feel good about. Celebrate our small successes. When someone gives us a complement, simply take a deep breath, smile and let it soak in.

Comparing
Do we compare ourselves to others? Comparing ourselves to others doesn't motivate us to do more or be better; instead, it makes us feel we'll never be good enough. Recognize our uniqueness. We are one of a kind, and there is no one in the universe like us. Make a list of words that describe our uniqueness; begin to create a list of adjectives that describe us - at least 25 positive words about our greatness.

Motivation
Motivation is the process that initiates, guides and maintains goal-oriented behaviors. Motivation is what causes us to act; it involves the biological, emotional, social and cognitive forces that activate behavior. Simply put, we make time and effort for the things we want to do.

When it comes to weight loss, motivation is something that is sometimes hard to have enthusiasm for.

What is motivation? There are three components:
- Activation
- Persistence
- Intensity

Activation is the decision to start a behavior; *I want to lose weight.*

Persistence is the effort we put toward the behavior; *I will commit to making positive changes to help me lose weight.*

Intensity is the concentration and the passion put behind achieving a goal; *I will make five positive choices per day towards my goal to lose weight*

Finding motivation
When we want to make a change and know we need to make a change, but are increasing in resistance instead of willingness, how do we stay motivated to lose weight?
- Be honest with ourselves – if you know we are not going to be motivated right away to start exercising, do something else that we feel we would be more inspired to do like making healthier food choices. Then work our way up to exercise.
- Be positive – every step we take toward improving our health is a good step. Stay optimistic and believe in ourselves.
- Be patient – some things may not work right away, but give it time to work itself out.
- Be flexible – some days we won't be as motivated as others, acknowledge how we feel and do the best we can to stay on track.

Martyrdom
Being a martyr is how we justify self-sacrificing behaviors as something honorable and valiant. In reality, all we are

saying is everything and everyone is more important to us than us.

"I can't switch to healthier foods because my kids really like hot dogs and French fries."

"I put in a lot of hours at the office; I don't have time to exercise."

"People depend on me, and I need to be there for them."

Sound familiar? If we find ourselves making unnecessary sacrifices for the "greater good," ask ourselves what good we would be to those who rely on us if we were unable to function. If we are not good to ourselves, we are no good to anyone.

Remember, we are our most valuable possession.

All or nothing
Do we only see things in black and white and not shades of gray? Do things have to be one way or the other with no room for negotiation? Sometimes having an "all or nothing" attitude is beneficial; however, when it comes to healthier lifestyle changes, it can be a deterrent.

Lifestyle changes done in increments may be helpful to making them become permanent habits. Piling on too much can be overwhelming, some things may suffer in the process, and we may be more likely to give up.

To break us from an "all or nothing" approach to weight loss, remember:

- Some is better than none
- We are not in a race
- Work smarter, not harder

100   I Know How to Lose Weight, So Why Haven't I?

Mind games can cause major road blocks to weight loss. The games we play are usually manifestations of bigger issues.

When we notice we are playing games with our weight loss success, take some time to deal with the issue that is preventing us from moving forward.

10

The quick-fix

You can't take a fast food approach to a healthy lifestyle

The quick-fix comes in when we try to achieve maximum results in minimal time. Upcoming special events, vacations, or one day we look in the mirror and ask ourselves, "How did I get like this?" We know we need to do something, but we do not know where to start or even *how* to start.

We set a date to take action, but that date is now a week past due. One late night while snacking in front of the T.V., we see a commercial with a trim, toned, bronzed woman running on the beach with a buff companion. She states that she has lost 15 lbs in 14 days by just taking a pill! "That's what I have been waiting for" we say to ourselves, ignoring our own common sense telling us that we cannot believe everything we see on television.

Or we're surfing our social media feeds and we see hourglass-shaped women or reality celebrities promoting waist trainers and diet teas. Or our friend at the job sends us an e-mail about the latest diet that promises we can lose 30 lbs in a month if we eat lemon peels before every meal. As irrational as it sounds, we can always find someone that swears it works, they know a friend of a friend who tried it and convinces us that it is worth a try.

When we follow fad diets that encourage calorie restrictions or deprivation, we may encounter some weight loss. However, when the goal weight is achieved and we go back to our regular eating habits, we usually wind up back at our pre-diet weight plus a few extra pounds.

Why Diets Don't Work
For one "die" is in the first part of the word. This is appropriate because, most of the time when we are on a diet, we feel like we are going to die waiting for it to be over.

Diets are based on restrictions and abstaining from foods we love to eat. Just the thought of going on a diet builds up resistance in our bodies that actually makes losing weight more difficult.

The whole time we are denying ourselves the foods we want, all we can focus on is when the diet will be over and getting back to eating regularly.

"Lose 14 lbs in 10 days!"

"Drop a dress size in one hour!"

"The fastest fat burner on the market!"

"Eat this, drink this, take this and watch the pounds melt away."

We are bombarded with these messages and promises of quick and easy. We subscribe to the quick-fix because it does not require much effort.

Instead, we will put our faith and money into any pill, powder or diet plan that promises to perform fast.

There are many pills on the market that are endorsed to be effective in burning fat and raising metabolism, and even have clinical studies on record to back up those claims.

However, a lot of these pills contain ingredients that could be harmful to our bodies. We tend to put too much faith and not enough good sense in the effectiveness of diet pills and should avoid them altogether.

If we have ever taken the time to read the labels on most of the diet pills on the market, we will notice one common disclaimer, "For best results drink plenty of water, eat a well-balanced meal, and exercise 20 minutes a day at least three days per week."
Hmmm... that makes us wonder where the pill comes into play.
If we removed the quick-fix crutch and followed the disclaimer instead, wouldn't we still lose weight? Not as fast, we may be thinking.

When dealing with weight loss, fast is not always better. It took time cultivating the bad habits to get us where we are now; trying to undo that in 14 days could cause more harm than good.

When we lose weight too fast the loss is usually from water and muscle tissue. The last thing we want to lose is muscle! Muscle tissue helps to burn fat. The more muscle mass we have, the more calories we burn.

People that lose weight too fast do appear smaller, but they tend to still look round and have no real definition or tone to their body. Someone who loses weight more slowly and steadily with proper nutrition and exercise has more tone and definition and an overall healthier appearance.

The quick-fix can also be defined as doing too much too soon. "If I workout really hard every day, I'll reach my goal faster!" Out the gate, we hit our workouts hard, pushing ourselves to complete exhaustion.

Then after a few weeks we feel a sharp pain in our knee or ankle or some other part of our bodies. We decide to give our bodies a rest day. However, our bodies need more rest, and that day turns into a week, then into a month. Then, we realize it's been six months or more since we've worked out.

There are a few ways to unlearn the quick-fix mentality. Instead of opting for the quick fix approach:

- Be realistic. Anything that seems too good to be true usually is. As much as we want to believe that we can look good in a bikini in 14 days just by taking a pill, we have to realize that anything worth having is worth working for.

- Do not wait until the last minute. When we let special occasions and holidays creep up on us, we tend to look for the quickest way possible to reach our goals. We place a lot of unhealthy mental and physical stress on ourselves mainly because we are worried about what others will think. Do not put unnecessary pressure on ourselves to look a certain way or to be a certain size for an event. I, personally, think that causes more anxiety than motivation to reach one's goal.

- When the decision to change is ours and the timeframe in which to reach a goal is one that is made on our own terms, we have the control over how and when our goal will be reached.

There is no quick-fix to lifestyle change. In reality, it took time to gain the weight and it is going to take time to lose it. If we take time to lose it properly, it will remain off. Learning to eat properly and in moderation may take more time to yield results than a fad diet, but the results will be easier to maintain permanently. There is no magic solution for weight loss.

Building a better body is like building a house. The plan has to be laid out with all the details and the blueprint has to be drawn before construction can even begin. You have to start with the foundation and framework, and then add on to it until the house is completed. If we try to rush the process or cut corners, we set ourselves up for major problems. If done properly we can enjoy that house for years with very little maintenance or upkeep.

106 I Know How to Lose Weight, So Why Haven't I?

11

Looking good
=
Feeling good

Self-worth does not lie in our dress size, it lies within us.

One day while out shopping, we find an outfit we love and try it on in our usual size; but it doesn't fit right. We really love the outfit, but refuse to buy it in a larger size.

Size tags are just guidelines based on average body measurements.

I don't know how many times I have heard women (myself included) say they would not buy themselves clothes until they lost weight. When we see someone in a nice outfit we do not say, "That is a nice outfit, what size is it?" For one, that would be rude. Size does not matter if the person looks good.

We can all relate to having the right outfit on with the right accessories, hair nicely coiffed, and makeup flawless. When we know we look good, no one can tell us different.

There is absolutely no logic in obsessing over size tags and placing so much self-worth in them.

Some would say having an outfit in our goal size can serve as motivation. Size tags are just guidelines and are not predictors of success. What if we never get to that goal size? Success is measured by how we look and feel. If we can buy an outfit and not feel self-conscious about what is hanging where, I would say that is success no matter what size that outfit is.

Looking good and feeling good is not something that depends on our weight. Looking good is something we can do now to feel good about ourselves. First, get rid of the clothes we have that do not fit.

Make the commitment to stop torturing ourselves and making ourselves feel insecure by wearing clothing that is uncomfortable and too small. Go through our closets. If we have not worn an outfit in over a year, assume we will not wear it.

Clothing is meant to be worn. Donate our old outfits to charity. There are many homeless people and people who are coming off of welfare and trying to get employment that need nice clothing. We will be helping those less fortunate, as well as ourselves.

Makeovers on talk shows are the best example of this: taking a regular person, giving them a new hairstyle, some makeup and a flattering outfit. We see the person transform before our eyes; not just from the outside but the inside as well.

Taking pride in our appearance conveys self-love and that we feel like a worthy person who takes care of herself/himself.

Create a signature look. Give ourselves a makeover. Get together with a good friend (one who will give us an honest opinion) and go shopping. Try different clothing styles; go to trendy shops that carry the latest fashions. Create different looks for different activities: business, casual, workout, and evening.

Experiment with colors we are not used to wearing. If we are not sure if we should buy an outfit, take a picture of ourselves in it. If it looks good on us, go for it! Try a new hairstyle or hair color. For those who wear glasses and want to try contacts, try them. Improving the way we look now will boost self-confidence. A neglected outward appearance is a sure sign things are not right within.

YouTube is a great resource for fashion, hair and makeup tutorials. There are women of all shapes, sizes, hair types and skin tones that can assist us in finding a look that may work for us.

Don't punish ourselves by waiting until we reach our weight loss goal to invest in our appearance. Looking our best will help us feel our best.

As I look down at the jeans I have on and see the bulge hanging over my waistband that is pushing up the rolls on my sides, I think about the constant tugging, pulling, tucking and adjusting I am going to be doing all day.

I have to laugh. I bought these jeans at a deep discount store for less than $20.00. They are an irregular size 14. From day one, they did not fit comfortably, but I am determined to get the most out of my minimal investment.

Instead of giving the jeans away or exchanging them for a larger size, I torture myself by squeezing into these uncomfortable jeans and spending the rest of the day feeling self-conscious, with my arms crossed trying to hide the rolls on my stomach.

"Why?" I have to ask myself. I know the answer- the size tag says 14.

As punishment for this, I force myself to wear these jeans as a constant reminder of what a failure I am. How dare I gain so much weight! I do not deserve to buy new clothes.

Forget the fact that they are irregular jeans, thus explaining why they were in a deep discount store. They are a size 14!

Does that sound rational to you?.... Me either.

12

Maintenance

If healthier living is going to be a lifestyle, it has to last a lifetime.

It is not too early to put a maintenance plan in place. Develop maintenance strategies for those days when we may find ourselves slipping back into bad habits. This way, we will not wait until the damage is done, we will be able to catch ourselves before we fall. Here are a few ideas:

- Plan ahead for holidays and other occasions where we may tend to slip.
- Plan non-food related outings with friends.
- Be an inspiration to others. If we know someone that is where we were, take them under our wing and help them achieve their personal fitness goal; this will help us remain active and involved in maintaining our own fitness achievement.

We may notice that as we progress those around us may start behaving differently as a result of the new us. It will not be because we have changed and become obnoxious; it will be because we make people that are still stuck in old patterns feel insecure.

Seek friendships with people, who like ourselves, want to live happier, healthier lives. This helps to maintain a healthy lifestyle.

Try doing the things we have put off due to low self-image. Although these things should have been explored earlier in our transformation process, there is always one thing that we have said to ourselves we would do, "once I get my weight under control."

For some, maintaining weight loss takes as much work as it did to lose the weight because they opted for the quick-fix. By taking slower, well-planned steps in the weight loss process, we have made healthy choices an integrated part of our daily life, with every component strategically plotted to fit our schedule.

Be realistic with our maintenance plan. If there are components of our current workout and eating plan we don't like, make changes that will be easier for us to follow.

Falling off track
We have a bad day. We over-indulge during the holidays. One late night out with friends has us sleeping in the next day and the day after. One day of inactivity turns into one week, then one month. The next thing we know, it's been months since we've worked out or ate properly.

Falling off track happens; the key is to catch ourselves before too much time passes. Taking an assessment (included in chapter 6) regularly (every three months) will help us stay on track.

Realize that proper nutrition, staying active, hydrated and getting enough sleep are non-negotiable when it comes to maintaining a healthy lifestyle.

Schedules change, life circumstances evolve and physical needs change. We have to be flexible and make adjustments accordingly.

Assess what went wrong and strategize ways to prevent those setbacks from happening again. Maybe we need to take more time developing good habits. Maybe we need to find a better support system. Maybe we are dealing with saboteurs and need to change our circle. Maybe we are the saboteur, and we need to find out why we are sabotaging ourselves.

The key to overcoming falling off track is to not spend time beating ourselves up. Assess, adjust and get back in the game. Learn from our mistakes, and love ourselves through it all!

Follow online:

Blog:
www.lmeceo.com

Facebook:
@lisamevansceo

Twitter:
@lisamevansceo
#IKHLW

Instagram:
@lisamevansceo

YouTube:
Lisamevansceo

#IKHLW

#loveyourselfbacktogoodhealth

Afterword

Of all the issues that face our society, weight is still one of the biggest (no pun intended). With fast-paced schedules and endless responsibilities, we tend to go through our days on autopilot; choosing a lifestyle of convenience over one of substance. I hope, through this book, you have at least learned to slow down and take a few moments to take a realistic look at your present state. To learn that you are not alone and things are not as hopeless as you may think they are.

Getting started on the road to change is never easy. However, if you take time to map out your route, you make the journey more pleasurable and learn to navigate around the roadblocks. I would love to hear about your journey. Tell me of your experiences, and let me know where this book can be improved. I wish you much success in all of your endeavors. Follow me on Twitter and Instagram @lisamevansceo

Good Luck,

Lisa M. Evans

I hope you enjoyed reading this book
I would appreciate it if you would be kind enough to go to Amazon and leave a review

Amazon review link:
https://www.amazon.com/Know-How-Lose-Weight-Havent-ebook/product-reviews/B06X41DMLB/ref=cm_cr_dp_d_show_all_top?ie=UTF8&reviewerType=all_reviews

Again, thank you very much for reading my book and remember to love yourself back to good health

Notes

Notes

Glossary

A

action - the manner or method of performing

activity - the quality or state of being active

anxiety- a painful or apprehensive uneasiness of mind usually over and impending or anticipated ill

B

boredom - the state of being weary and restless through lack of interest

C

calorie - a unit equivalent to the large calorie expression heat-producing or energy-producing value in food when oxidized in the body

change - to give a different position, course, or direction to

contro l - to exercise restraining or directing influence over

D

dehydration - an abnormal depletion of body fluids

depression - a psychoneurotic or psychotic disorder marked especially by sadness, inactivity, difficulty in thinking and concentration, a significant increase or decrease in appetite and time spent sleeping, feelings of dejection and hopelessness, and sometimes suicidal tendencies

diet - food and drink regularly provided or consumed

digestion - the process of making food absorbable by dissolving it and breaking it down into simpler chemical compounds that occurs in the living body

E

energy - the capacity of acting or being active

F

failure - a state of inability to perform a normal function

fat - well filled out; plump; obese

fitness - the quality or state of being fit

food - material consisting essentially of protein, carbohydrate, and fat used in the body of an organism to sustain growth, repair, and vital processes and to furnish energy

G

goal - the end toward which effort is directed

guilt - feelings of culpability especially for imagined offences or from a sense of inadequacy

H

health - the condition of being sound in mind, body, or spirit

I

injury - an act that damages or hurts

M

metabolism - the chemical changes in living cells by which energy is provided for vital processes and activities

motivation - the condition of being motivated; incentive; drive

muscle - a body tissue consisting of long cells that contract when stimulated and produce motion

N

nutrition - the act or process of nourishing or being nourished

P

pescetarian - a pescetarian diet excludes land animals and birds, but includes fish, mollusks, and crustaceans in addition to fruits, vegetables, plants, legumes, nuts, and grains. Eggs and dairy may or may not be present in the pescetarian's diet.

permanent - continuing or enduring without fundamental or marked change

physical - concerned or preoccupied with the body and its needs

positive - having or expressing actual existence or quality as distinguished from deprivation or deficiency

Q

quick - inclined to hastiness

R

results - beneficial or tangible effect

routine - a regular course of procedure

S

schedule - a written or printed list, catalogue, or inventory

strategy - a careful plan or method

V

vegan - a vegetarian who omits all animal products from the diet

W

weight - relative heaviness; mass

Index

A
action, 15, 16, 90, 101
activity, 25, 59, 64, 65, 90
age, 5, 49
Alcohol, 26, 27, 45
anxiety, 16, 45, 73, 88, 89, 91, 105

B
body, 16, 24, 25, 40, 41, 43, 44, 45, 49, 55, 60, 61, 62, 63, 68, 69, 72, 85, 102, 105, 107
boredom, 82

C
caffeine, 23, 24, 25, 26, 41, 45
calorie, 26, 27, 102
calories, 23, 25, 26
change, 15, 16, 21, 54, 62, 73, 81, 84, 86, 90, 91, 105, 115
control, 44, 54, 81, 85, 89, 105, 112

D
dehydration, 41, 42
depression, 36, 86, 93
diet, 6, 25, 39, 45, 48, 50, 80, 90, 101, 103, 105
digestion, 24, 40, 41

E
easy, 54, 103, 115
eat, 24, 25, 26, 27, 40, 48, 49, 50, 79, 80, 101, 103, 105
energy, 23, 24, 25, 33, 43, 73

F
failure, 15, 16, 21
fat, 15, 24, 40, 50, 102, 103, 115
feelings, 35, 36, 41, 74, 80, 81, 85, 86, 89, 91
fitness, 35, 63, 64, 89, 111, 119
food, 16, 24, 25, 40, 48, 49, 54, 80, 81, 111
friends, 74, 111
function, 23, 35, 40, 50

G
goal, 5, 33, 36, 37, 64, 81, 88, 89, 91, 102, 105, 108, 111
guilt, 35, 88, 89, 91

H
habit, 23, 24, 68, 69, 100
health, 39, 41, 86, 120
healthy, 50, 68, 102, 112

I
injury, 60, 63, 64

M
maintenance, 5, 105, 111
metabolism, 24, 103
motivation, 15, 89, 105, 108
muscle, 40, 41, 49, 68, 102

N
Nutrition, 117, 120

P

permanent, 15, 16, 41, 54, 84, 104, 105
physical, 15, 16, 41, 43, 59, 80, 84, 105
pills, 103
plan, 16, 35, 37, 80, 90, 91, 103, 105, 111
positive, 24, 36, 73, 81, 85
Positive, 23, 85

Q

quick, 16, 21, 64, 72, 101, 103, 104, 105

R

results, 101, 103, 105
roadblock, 84, 88
routine, 16, 37, 41, 45, 64

S

schedule, 35, 44, 45, 90, 112
self-confidence, 109
Self-worth, 107
serving, 25, 26, 49, 54
size, 49, 103, 105, 107, 108, 110
sleep, 24, 25, 39, 43, 44, 45, 46, 62
strategy, 16, 31, 80, 91
stress, 16, 44, 84, 85, 105
Sunlight, 45

W

weight, 5, 6, 8, 15, 16, 23, 26, 36, 39, 40, 48, 54, 59, 60, 61, 63, 64, 79, 80, 86, 88, 89, 90, 100, 104, 105, 107, 108, 112, 115, 117

Colophon

Research and Gathering
Web: Mozilla Firefox
Art: Lisa Evans
Photos: iPhone 6S, Target portrait studio
Scanning: HP-Desk Jet 2400 series.

Writing and manuscript building
Manuscript preparation: MS-Word 2007
Typesetting: MS-Word 2007
    Body text: Century gothic, 10pt
    Headers: Verdana, 10pt
    Chapter titles: Century gothic BT, 26 pt
    Quotations: Century gothic italic BT, 12pt

Prepress
Copyediting and fact checking: Alissa Vaughn, La Toya Smith
Cover design by Lisa M. Evans

Conversion
MS-Word to PDF: Adobe Acrobat

Printing
Paper: 60# white offset book
Cover: 10pt C1S, four color, layflat film lamination, matte.
Binding: Perfect bound (adhesive, softcover)

126 I Know How to Lose Weight, So Why Haven't I?

www.ingramcontent.com/pod-product-compliance
Lightning Source LLC
Chambersburg PA
CBHW060516030426
42337CB00015B/1913